Things Are Big When You're A BUG

by Ken Marrs
Drawings by Mike Motz

For Nicholas and Emma
Adventure Awaits You!
Love, Daddy

Order this book online at www.trafford.com/08-0033

or email orders@trafford.com

Most Trafford titles are also available at major online book retailers.

© Copyright 2008 Ken Marrs.

All rights reserved. No part of this publication may be reproduced, stored in a retrieval system, or transmitted, in any form or by any means, electronic, mechanical, photocopying, recording, or otherwise, without the written prior permission of the author.

Note for Librarians: A cataloguing record for this book is available from Library and Archives Canada at www.collectionscanada.ca/amicus/index-e.html

Printed in Victoria, BC, Canada.

ISBN: 978-1-4251-6840-7

We at Trafford believe that it is the responsibility of us all, as both individuals and corporations, to make choices that are environmentally and socially sound. You, in turn, are supporting this responsible conduct each time you purchase a Trafford book, or make use of our publishing services. To find out how you are helping, please visit www.trafford.com/responsiblepublishing.html

Our mission is to efficiently provide the world's finest, most comprehensive book publishing service, enabling every author to experience success. To find out how to publish your book, your way, and have it available worldwide, visit us online at www.trafford.com/10510

www.trafford.com

North America & international
toll-free: 1 888 232 4444 (USA & Canada)
phone: 250 383 6864 ♦ fax: 250 383 6804
email: info@trafford.com

The United Kingdom & Europe
phone: +44 (0)1865 722 113 ♦ local rate: 0845 230 9601
facsimile: +44 (0)1865 722 868 ♦ email: info.uk@trafford.com

10 9 8 7 6 5 4 3 2

Billy Bunglebug was bored,
A frown upon his face;
"There's nothing here to do", he snored,
And moped about the place.

Billy huffed; "I've seen it all!
Gone as far as I can go...
I run and run, but I'm so small,
I'm never far from home!"

Mama Bug had heard this talk,
And mentioned with a grin;
"Papa's going to take a walk,
You should go with him."

"He's going to a People Place,
To gather us some crumbs;"
Papa said; "No time to waste,
If you would like to come!"

Betty rushed to pack her things;
A blanket, dress and brush.
Billy grabbed some toys to bring,
They all left in a rush.

They walked towards the edge of town,
And Papa walked so fast!
When nightfall came they all lay down,
And slept there in the grass.

When Billy woke, his legs were sore;
He missed his little bed.
He looked back where they'd been before;
"Our house is gone", he said.

This work was more than Billy liked;
The grass grew very tall.
It seemed no matter how they hiked,
They got nowhere at all!

Then suddenly they passed a rise,
And Billy stopped to stare.
What a wonderful surprise;
The People House was there!

Papa Bug then led them all,
Quietly down the hill.
They followed Papa up the wall,
And through the windowsill.

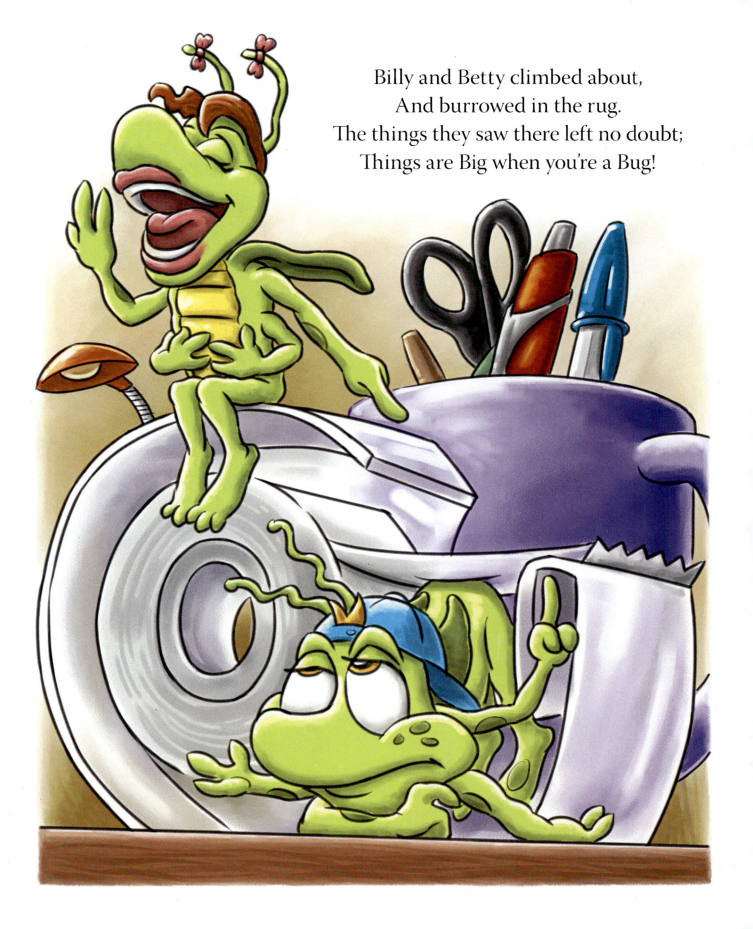

Billy and Betty climbed about,
And burrowed in the rug.
The things they saw there left no doubt;
Things are Big when you're a Bug!

They saw a chair, much like their own;
But taller than a tree!
It seemed the countertop had grown,
Too high to even see!

The walls stretched on for miles and miles;
The ceiling reached to space!
Billy wondered all the while;
What lived in such a place?

Then all at once they heard a sound;
A crashing, pounding din!
And just as Billy turned around,
A *Giant Thing* thumped in!

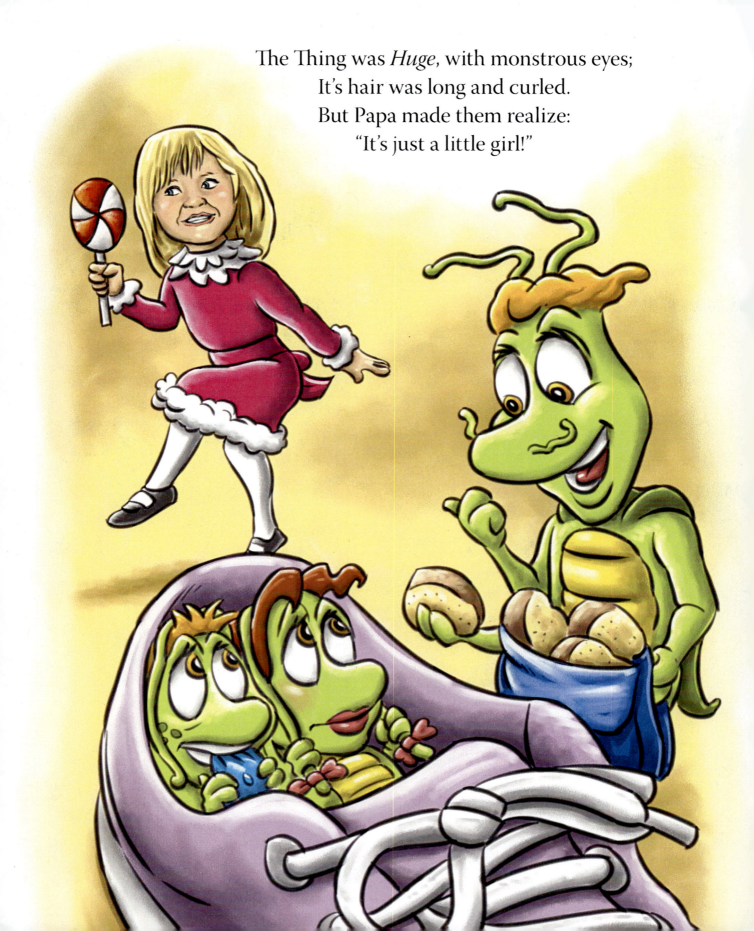

The Thing was *Huge*, with monstrous eyes;
It's hair was long and curled.
But Papa made them realize:
"It's just a little girl!"

The girl saw Billy on the rug,
And suddenly cried; "EEEK!"
"A bug! A bug! I see a BUG!"
And ran out with a shriek!

Papa rushed to gather crumbs,
Found on the kitchen floor.
When all the gathering was done,
They crept under the door.

The journey home took quite a while,
And as they neared the field,
Billy saw his sister smile;
"I see our house!" she squealed.

Both were glad to be at home,
And couldn't wait to tell their Ma;
About how far they all had roamed,
And all the wondrous things they saw!

As Billy slept in bed that night,
Tucked in all warm and snug,
He dreamed of all those giant sights;
Things Are Big When You're A Bug!

The End